# A CUSTOMISED SELECTION
# OF FIREWORKS

# PREVIOUS BOOKS BY DOMINIC FISHER

*The Ladies and Gentlemen of the Dead*, The Blue Nib, 2019

# A CUSTOMISED SELECTION OF FIREWORKS

## DOMINIC FISHER

Shoestring Press

Printed by imprintdigital
Upton Pyne, Exeter
www.digital.imprint.co.uk

Typesetting and cover design by The Book Typesetters
us@thebooktypesetters.com
07422 598 168
www.thebooktypesetters.com

Published by Shoestring Press
19 Devonshire Avenue, Beeston, Nottingham, NG9 1BS
(0115) 925 1827
www.shoestringpress.co.uk

First published 2022
© Copyright: Dominic Fisher
© Cover painting by Cathy Fisher
www.davidhigham.co.uk/authors-dh/cathy-fisher
www.facebook.com/CathyFisherArt

The moral right of the author has been asserted.

ISBN 978-1-915553-01-0

# ACKNOWLEDGEMENTS

Thanks are due to the editors of *The Blue Nib Magazine*, *Frosted Fire*, *The High Window*, *Locked Down* (Poetry Space Ltd, 2021), and *Raceme*, where some of these poems first appeared, to the producers of West Wilts Radio's *The Poetry Place*, who broadcast others, and to the organisers and judges of Cheltenham Poetry Festival's Wild Poems competition, and the Cinnamon Literature Award 2020, in which some of these poems were shortlisted.

Many thanks also to Matthew Barton, Colin Brown, Deborah Harvey, Helen Ivory, Dave Kavanagh, Richard Lance Keeble, and Chris Lindop for help and support, and to Cathy Fisher for the cover art.

For Chris and Robin

# CONTENTS

## *indoors*

## *and out*

indoors

# A CUSTOMISED SELECTION OF FIREWORKS

It's the sequence that really matters
  colour rhythm flow
which isn't something the lay person
  gets right every time.

Maybe start with deep frozen sparklers
  some St Anthony's fire
a few howling spiders, remembering
  odd numbers work best.

So, scotch bonnet, popcorn bombette
  high hats, puff adder
jammy dodgers, some gamboge, and
  a titanium salute.

Next one or two long-range screamers
  a tequilla sunrise
some bloody cranesbill followed by
  a fat green mamba.

Nearly there now with a gentle brocade
  three knee crackers
a will-o-the-whip then the *coup de grâce*
  a haemo-goblin.

Excellent. Would you like the receipt?
  Take care with my children.
Please light them only in darkness
  and enjoy the show.

# REPEAT PATTERN

You are making a blind for a window
working by the light of that same window

with metres of dandelions hanging
in folds off the sides of the ironing board.

Iron in one hand, cloth in the other
you shake straight a repeat-pattern meadow

which we'll raise on a chain in the mornings
drop like improbable suns at night.

This is no time to shut out the day, I know
and yet I want to close all curtains and blinds

then watch you standing among measurements
ironing a seam in a field of light.

# WAVES MOVING THROUGH A ROOM

As days have weight
so too do rooms

Their volumes
hum around you

as you sit at your table
write at your desk

take in waves from prisms
and cylinders plugged into a wall

And if shelves have their objects
the light upon them has pitch

Listen now to things on shelves
singing about the minutes

streaming among them
like shoals of fish

their own half-meanings
like birds on their lips

and to the room itself
weighty in the background

as cutlery clicks in your hands
as keys tap beneath your fingers

# CLOUD FORMATION

The first hour, no cloud
and a half moon still high
lays light through the window
like dust here on the floor
where I stand still asleep
in a part of myself.

Is this the perfect path
a way to take us through
these muddled hemispheres?
The moon is fading though
is shifting out toward
different times and countries.

There is no perfect path
nor any twisting road
just this other hour
with cloud forming between
wires branches houses
across the day now here.

# READING ALOUD FOR MRS KITE

Take the feather home and read it to yourself
                    she said.

It was a drawing of a feather
on the left
lines on white

with all the words about the feather
                              on the right.

So after tea you read them, with your mouth
                    and in your head.
Then you read aloud no doubt in class next day
                    for Mrs Kite.

What did they say, those words like feathers?
You suppose there were rhymes with *fly*
                              and *sky, bird*
                              or even *kite*

and because this was kindergarten, not *hawk*
                              or *dove*, not
                              *quill* or *flight*.

We pick up the feather       in that picture
on the left.                 then we write
on our uncertain page with mouth and head
                    for Mrs Kite.

# INDOOR FIREWORKS

Make it dark
switch off the lights
and draw the curtains.
          Listen
a scratch, a yellow spurt
then the blue base.
A fountain flows solo
in a winter park
goes gold, sputters.
          Listen
another match. A ruby fern
becomes a burning forest
goes grey and fractal.
          Switch on the light.
It's Christmas or his birthday.
The winter tea-time litter
momentarily strange
now includes a plate of cones
like burnt-out chocolates
among the mugs and cakes.
          Listen
how some smart remark
that set a bad example
to the younger children
is all it takes to set him off.
          Switch on the light
decades later, still forgetting
how easily a fuse is lit.
Make it dark again, watch
the sparks, the slow flame.
          Listen.

# INSECTS AND SPIDERS I

Italicised text from *Insects and Spiders*, H Trevor Jones,
Warne & Co, 1952

*Earwigs*

*Nocturnal creatures who seek some suitable cranny*
*in the daytime. They are perfectly harmless*
*despite the superstitions of those who ought to know*
*better.* Still, we kids knew very well how they bite

in the daytime. They are perfectly harmless
till they crawl in your ear and through to your brain.
Better still, we kids knew very well how they bite,
they nip you with bum-pincers as they climb your neck.

Till they crawl in your ear and through to your brain
you are safe, but call on Our Lady in case
they nip you with bum-pincers as they climb your neck.
Holy Mary, Mother of God, pray for us.

You are safe, but call on Our Lady in case.
Despite the superstitions of those who ought to know,
Holy Mary, Mother of God, pray for us
nocturnal creatures who seek some suitable cranny.

*Large Tortoiseshell*

*Reddish, brown-black, yellow and blue markings.*
*Under surface brown, marked like watered silk*
inside a wardrobe of forgotten wings.
*Reddish, brown-black, yellow and blue markings*
are shut now in the book with other things
from our supposed gold time of free school milk.
*Reddish, brown-black, yellow and blue markings.*
We were bruised back then, *marked like watered silk.*

*Moth in a bath*

Not found in the book
this drab quarter inch
half fish half silk hinge
twitching then resting
was there in the scum
all the same.

Still an altar boy
I did not question
that this slight creature
drowning unpublished
under its own shroud
was a moth of God
but I must confess
to clumsy fingers.

Yet as the wet wings
trailed vainly across
the rim of the bath
what green-gold came off
what a slick of grey
and purple scales
were revealed that way.

*Webs*

Mr H Trevor Jones wrote his two pages of spiders
            at night, I imagine, longhand
                     the ink like silk, a silver nib

*Garden spider*     *globe-shaped*     *bearing a white cross*
*Wolf spider*            *roams the fields*
*Zebra spider*    *on sunny walls and fences*
                    *stalks its prey*

Mr Jones drew all the pictures too

        He doesn't tell us
              if our mother was a spider

but he would have told me
        that even if a sister was screaming
it was mistaken to put house spiders out the window

I can see now
        the rickety latch, the smeary pane
          and a fat sun
              like a *silken cocoon*
                 in the elm in the field

can still see how, later
        the webs of outer space
           were thick with silver

# RED BIRD BLUES

*Amber*

Break-time toffee in its crinkled paper case
was so sweet and hard you licked your tongue sore.

You knew aged six or so how amber earrings must taste
like brown sugar, and one would take all day to suck.

Now you know if amber was diluted, all yellows
would proceed from it in gold yolky puddles,

that this evening will soon become a deluge
of fossil whiskies, resin, rivulets of tea.

And the sun coming down in pieces must be
all one monster storm-cycle of boiling ambers.

## Magenta

This is purple on acid
Satan having fun

what Jesus had in mind
turning water into wine

This is one third of all tone
on paper if not in fact

Without it there is no
singing no vibraphone

Take your lovely poison
put your cloak of opium on

Plug in a rose turn it up
enter the magenta zone

*Slate*

A night-time former slate-mining town,
its doorsteps as handsome as headstones.

No lights, no lock-in at The Black Lion,
the curtains are closed in B&B windows.

Only you and maybe shadows of cats
tread on the tarmac. At the top of the hill

the slab of sky is veined with quartz.
A hush of leaves, a dog barking below.

Here is the chapel, slates missing, but there still
handsome as doorsteps, are all its headstones.

*Cobalt blues*

Off the Atlantic
clouds roll in

swinging their tails
like a school of blue whales

sing deep as bells
on waves of light

in their indigo zone
in fathoms of sound

You stand in the downpour
a fall of dark water

of your blue silk dress
a delta of ink

Rivers run slow
till dawn when the gap

as we swim in the mines
in the curtains shines

*Red bird*

Tomorrow the forest will be grey,
streets ran red yesterday, today
a bird is singing in an elder bush.

The bird is thin, the song no rejoicing
but an urgent claim to territory.
All the same, today a bird is singing.

The calendars will burn and blow away.
And right now one red spark is singing
from its vantage on an elder bush.

# CAT GOES FROM ROOM TO ROOM

Spaces open up as invitations
to this young cat. Every surface
is accessible and magnificent
every object may be a foothold
and nothing goes unnoticed.

      She is yourself

in those dreams where you go
from room to unexpected room.
So here you come to a kitchen
long locked and forgotten, here
afternoon half covers a table
while out in the hall it's midwinter.

      When you get back

among the cables and candlesticks
of the room you started from
things aren't quite as you remember
but as you step along the shelves
every surface is accessible
every space inside another.

# WHITE BOX

This fridge
is a depository
of crusts and rinds
a secret facility of moulds
a tabernacle
of abandoned milk and butter.

It is grimy and flaccid
in the seal round its door.
It is vivid in what remains
in peeled-back plastic trays

fabulous with cold furs
clogged in its slots
thick with spatterings and seepage
swamped to an inch in the floor.

And I will clean it
make surfaces squeak
and shelves translucent.
with scalding water, disinfectant.

I will set about
this feast of self-neglect
here and now, not stop
until we have a white box
that shuts tight

on the bacon and cheese
the packets of sandwiches
you will put there again
and forget.

# NOCTURNES
*for AF*

There was always music in the kitchen
on her radio, and something on the boil,
dishcloths, cigarettes, a minor key.
Little talk though, no touch that I recall.

Music was our mother in a way.
It filled silences, helped drown out the priests.
It softened chores and was emotion
where none would come, made a kind of home.

But then music was her mother too.
She could hear the Chopin from her bedroom,
applause and laughter, clinking glasses
as her mother played to guests downstairs.

The universe vibrates. No other touch,
except the keys, no other resolutions.
Each of us is still one child unheard
and music was the mother of us all.

# FAST FOOD

*School milk*

You had to drink it
whether icky from the sun
or slushy with pale blue ice

You were told to use a straw
not neck it making it go
guk-guk-guk-guk-guk

So when your friend
jabbed your ribs
it went Pwusssshhh
But Miss i-wuzim!

*Egg beans and chips*

It's vinegar first
otherwise
it washes off the salt
as rain water might
whether softer malt
or chip-shop white

Let an egg be the sun
rising from the pan
beans become clouds
Sit, prepare your lips
watch the sun set
on still salty chips

## A pear

is one green gold weight
two owls side by side
next four slick white boats
or unfinished lutes

Then it's one wet plate
pips, stalk, the wet knife
and slack strings of fruit


## Calamares

If you hadn't died
I'd flash fry some squid
with finely chopped garlic
in smoking olive oil

Patatas bravas
sweet with paprika
big simple salad
Spanish dry white

I can't of course
because squid doesn't fry
across that great divide

*Porridge*

Made with milk
scooped into bowls
like blue half worlds

A sea of cream
encircles a soft
brown sugar island

The terrible power
of a spoon


*The return of Odysseus*

When that brute Odysseus
finally made it home disguised
it wasn't a scar from hunting
his old nurse first recognised him by
but how he helped himself to olives
by the handful like a greedy child

# CAPTAIN HOOK SHOWS OFF THE NEW KITCHEN

Come on in. What do you think?
Swanky eh? But do be candid.
Oiled oak worktops, Belfast sink.
And all these gadgets work one-handed.

So if I untwizzle my old hook
then slot in this fancy blade
and turn it on – hamburger, look.
Who said piracy never paid?

Meringues? You swap this for this,
egg-white, sugar, gently whisk it,
nice low heat – a piece of piss.
While we're waiting have a biscuit.

I came ashore at last a winner
hence posh new kitchen, somewhat niche.
But you'll be wondering what's for dinner?
A jug of rum and then a quiche.

# HALFWAY DOWN THE STAIRS

Other people have lived there
a long time now, people with cash
who could have the walls painted white
get some scaffolding up to the roof.

You could imagine cream sofas
non-representational artworks
which our father, flat broke
and wrathful, would have scoffed at.

But tonight it's all stripped back
to mould-speckled plaster.
Our ruptured chairs
our dust-clogged rugs are gone.

Where the hall stand was
is a space I can see from here
stuffed with prayer books and gloves
smelling of bindings and wool.

The portraits have departed.
And forgive us our trespasses
this is the step where I made a ghost
and now where a howling starts

that sounds like a dog
left in the attic, that sticks
in my throat, halfway down
where I was remembering figures

who have fled from their landscapes
those who trespass against us
the words now deep in the walls,
this step where I once made a ghost.

# INSIDE

Shepton Mallet Prison, National Poetry Day 2019

The word and the law
a hand and the blame
the logic of locks
and meanings of keys
all come to the same.
Inside is this side
outside is not.

Venus or Mars or a plane
a gull in the last of day
these are no more
than pictures on walls.
Someone is shouting
on another floor.
Footsteps go down to the hall.

You can consider
how the world divides
or what freedoms could be
inside the inside
but you come to a door
locked on the side you don't see
when they put you inside.

# BLABBERHEAD

Sometimes you'll sit down beside me and say
        you have devolved to a fish
        swum into the glass of the window
        and away

Or you'll enunciate
        petrochemical   postbox
        tiger-moth   tight-rope
        abstention   portmanteaux

There may be announcements
        I sleep next to your sleep
        your mother and father have melted
        the larder is unlit and empty

Then you go quiet

as if someone had just left the room
or a machine had stopped running

You trickle back in
        Victoria sponge
        tangential   Eucharist
        interface   drain-pipe

No wisdoms, nothing I had forgotten

        we're in this together
        a thousand pianos

        delta
        unbroken skyline

# A DOUBLE ESPRESSO IN WOODES

Yes of course, have a seat, though please
don't start telling me last night's dreams.
I was there, for instance I know you found
yourself swimming into the centre of town.

Your hat is my hat, my house is your home.
We share the same fixed ideas, same shoes
same well upholstered contraption of bones.
I know what you think, know what you hope.

But this morning I'd wanted to be on my own,
to think nothing. Because this dark little pool
in a plain white cup is a kind of silence to me.
Never mind, you're here now, so sit down.

I don't know when the monsters will leave
when the ghosts will stop crowding our table.
I'm hoping it's soon, and I was, I suppose,
planning to wait quietly till then, avoid trouble

watch the world roll up and down Park Street
making it seem as if things never changed
as if it was only me here at the table, and we
had but one reflection and only one name.

# FACING A MIRROR

You walk into an ordinary room
           catch sight of another
where the wind is flat
           sunshine ricochets
letters turn back and
           books start at their endings

You face both ways
           across your own skin
you see windows
           in the wet of your eyeballs
thin blood tributaries
           one figure in each black pond

You ask yourself
           how you might pass through
a four millimetre
           thickness of glass

where half of eternity hangs
           in a sheet of silver
and your double vibrates
           when you cry or sing

where you will both vanish
           if you turn out the light
snap back into being
           if you switch it back on

And then you remember
           the boy by a pool
           who drank his reflection

# AUDIOLOGY

Bramble-tongued, beaks like scissors
their blind thickets stinking of fox
these are the same night birds
that sang the child you were to sleep.

Beetles rummaging in the brainpan
pipistrelles all but out of earshot
might be pinpointed, identified
placed on a scale from one to five.

No audiologist though
however kind or well equipped
could measure or detect
this bubbling of faraway throats.

But these unrecorded species are
still singing you toward the dark
through long unreachable summers
and the swift afternoons of winter.

# NOT QUITE MYSELF

Like you, I am vague sometimes
half in myself half out of it
like a shadow in a doorway.

I guess I am most myself asleep
though it can seem I'm underneath
a pile of other people's overcoats.

And even then I can hear the wind
rattling around outside going
*give us names let us in let us in*

*so we too can be solid citizens.*
*Let us inhabit your rooms, let us*
*press your buttons, wear your labels.*

I try to reply through the keyhole
but my mouth is locked, or a dog
has placed its paws across my face.

You shake me awake, *you're shouting*
you say. I try to explain but, like you
I'm not entirely myself at times.

# IN LOCKDOWN

your back gate is half open        in lockdown
the sun has stunned next door's grass    in lockdown
hedges and trees are opening their billion green hands

in lockdown     the lift is afraid
in lockdown     the stairways are panicky
both kids at once want your phone to call their friend

in lockdown     birds cross our windows in lockdown
the sky outside is drinkable blue     in lockdown
the night is peopled its moons familiar and you wake

in lockdown     each night-map turns and forgets us
in lockdown     I think I see you come round the corner
to whistles and pans and doors unlocking their hands

and out

# BONFIRE NIGHT FROM A LOFT WINDOW

As if street lights had detached themselves
to rise toward a surface we can't see

As if the traffic lights had broken loose
and detonated over town

As if a tree could stutter briefly into being
lose all its leaves then vaporise

As if windows in the tower blocks
were drifting off like spores

As if there might be trolls out there
popping bits of bubble wrap

As if there was a golden army coming
across the playing fields and now the roofs

As if angels saints and saddhus
had crashed your party with saxophones and bagpipes

As if the Reformation was no more than an evening out
with Popish gold and glass still drifting down

As if the fallout from the Government exploding
was a shower of banknotes on the hideouts of the homeless

As if setting fire to money
turned it into heavy-metal overhead

Then as if the TV screen had been switched off
the martyrs had burnt out crowds gone home

And gamelans gongs pots and pans
had ceased and everyone had gone to bed

But then as if they started up again
those half-remembered histories those untethered city lights

As if nodding off you had become
the house that you were watching from

As if the free-jazz drummer
raging over town might never stop

# THE HAYMARKET

The Rev Charles Wesley MA of Christchurch Oxford
is not buried here, stands at railings that were not there
and looks or does not look down on The Haymarket here.

*Radstock  Bath     Keynsham            Weston-super-Mare via Backwell*
*Brunel Doors      Sorry not in service           Park and Ride*

As he stands in the daffodils this cold spring and hears
or does not hear or see *vain the stone, the watch, the seal*
of all the graves once here only one is behind him now.

*London Has Fallen            Come Holy Ghost our hearts inspire*
*Precision Access Scaffolding           Express yourself*

Charles Wesley grips the railings with the dead behind him
hears *unlock the truth, thyself the key, unseal the sacred book*
as we watch vans and buses through the café windows.

*The South West Falcon        City Centre        Depots nationwide*

Wesley reads or does not read the words we see going past us,
flickers in and out between the buses. People chitter
on the pavements round The Haymarket and The Horsefair.

Plate-glass windows shake with the weight of passing wheels
*Ten thousand to their endless home/ this solemn moment fly*
Beneath the tarmac – former fields, water courses, other wheels.

*John, Martha Maria, Susannah, Selina, John James*
*Sarah his wife*

Standing in the daffodils gripping the railings
sitting here at big plate-glass windows
watching the words on the buses.

# THE SEAL-MAN

Out of the water was almost as wet as in it
that late afternoon when I came up the channel
on a spring tide in the singing of an on-shore wind
to look like a man, to speak and stand on the land.

I swam past the docks and under both motorways
in the muddled gush at the mouth of the river
hauled out on a kerbside and walked into town.
They let me be, on the bus. They thought I was drunk.

When I got there she was watching a film on TV
but her cry at the door sounded half like a seal.
*I kept my word* I said as she hung up my skin
like a big wet old coat, cursed me, then clung like a pup.

Her dad and her brothers would kill me she reckoned.
It took a while to talk them round, and sometimes
I noticed her mum watching me sideways still
but one way or another they got used to me.

Her mate's boyfriend was a roofer. He needed a hand.
I did fine. I could lug tiles up a ladder all day.
The trouble was up there I could see the bridges
and I could smell the sea in the rivers of air.

We were having a row. *Why can't you commit?* she asked.
*I'm a sea creature* I told her, *I came from the waves.*
She kind of understood me, went very quiet and said
*Well, there's another sea-creature inside me now.*

And I felt the tug of salt water right there and then
the smack and whisper of its long conversations
its booming quiet below, the colony calling.
*So swim with us* I said to the sea in her eyes.

*We'll slip through weed froth at the mud-blind fringes*
*into clear cold current.* She said *I'm bloody pregnant*
*I've got work in the morning, and I don't like boats.*
I told her the waves would rock us without any boat.

And day by day I saw I'd lost her. She drifted
further and darker inland on the words in her mouth.
I can't recall them exactly. Her mum was right
I was strange. I might as well swim down the river.

So here I am, heading that way. And how will it go?
Round in the circles the moons make I suppose.
I'll walk out of town, like some bloke in a big old coat
dodge through a fence at the side of the road and away.

But, before long, a child who asks too many questions
will stare out to sea with her toes in the foam
will be gone, swimming unseen like a seal, leaving
her nan going hysterical the length of the beach.

# EXCUSE ME SIR

Have you seen my mother and father?
Mr and Mrs Williams? That's our name
Williams, there in lovely letters
above my bed. That's me, Mary
though they call me Molly.
Our house is by St Philip's Marsh
back across the river where they lost me.
Mum is Alice, Dad is John
Mum does sewing, Dad goes up the ironworks.
The lady in the little house across the path
says they're waiting at the gates
but they aren't and I can't get through.
I see Mr Patten sometimes
who collects the sewing on a Friday.
Mum says how that's funny
a Mr Patten and the sewing.
I don't reckon he can see me
though I freeze when he comes. He whispers.
*What're you doing there Molly Williams*
*are you catching fishes, is it cold?*
Cold and quick as knives but thick
as mutton broth down on the bottom.
Angels like the stone ones came and caught me
*Sleep Molly till you rise with the just.*
But I wake up, like the boy next door
though all he says is *What's for dinner*
*what's for dinner, what's for dinner?*
I beg your pardon ma'am
have you seen my mother or my father?

# LUNCHTIME DRINKING

He was one end of the bar in a mackintosh
side-on to the ash-trays and woodwork
*A pint of old, if you don't mind, please John*
his back to nicotine-stained anaglypta
as he told those listening how in the army
they used to heat boot polish and sniff it.
He was thin and diffident, didn't seem
much like a soldier. The landlady made
corned-beef and pickle, cheese and onion
in white bread, or brown if you wanted.

A hundred miles distant, and a decade
later at least, you saw him again
standing stock-still on a roundabout
staring across a space where underpasses
and drinkers meet, the traffic slowing
and surging around him. The lights changed
you drove on, he was lost from view.

You can still hear coins rattling inside
the cigarette machine on the opposite wall
hear its yank-open slam-shut dispensers
still see a jar of eggs like boiled eyeballs
in clear vinegar there on the bar.

# MAKING WORDS FOR BREAD

He was squatting on a bundle
by the bakery, a jar
and a walking stick beside him.
On a board unpractised letters
inches high, said *I have no house*.
He looked like your father, but then
it wasn't English when he spoke.
So you both stood at the window
to make another language there
coining with your hands *eat* and *loaf*.

Much later, in your head, he said
in Damascus I had a house.
Damascus, where seven gates
see all of it, the trade and war
streets now like shattered bone,
that we have no father guiding us
and stars know nothing but themselves.
But still I got here though it was
to beg outside a bakery
without the words I need for bread.

# THE GOD IN THE TREE

I saw the dead clamber out of their boxes
spit out the mud, re-form from their ashes
kiss air and scramble their pieces together
for one last time to play musical instruments
in pubs for loose change and spend it on beer.

I saw the living climb into graveyards
eating the earth there or turning to ashes.
They drank the wind like draughts of poison
were dismantled by words in songs that seemed
to be only the names of flowers.

I followed the youthful the beautiful ageing
as they walked past shop windows and mirrors
handing out verses from boxes of light
seeming unaware I was there, that I knew them
that I knew every word they had written.

And I saw the rich on multiple platforms
weep as they tried to return a percentage
but no one would take it or help them
buy back the forests, resettle the cities
untangle outcomes never intended.

I saw the world's ending, every scenario
you didn't imagine. The cyborgs, the robots
the zombie diseases were nowhere in sight
but end it did as it always does
when I saw it beginning again.

And I watched the beginning again
all as you might imagine. The ice wolf
drawing its jaws back, valleys of rattling scree
that flushed with green, alphabets flourishing
wooden ships that freighted the seeds of the end.

All this time I hung from a balding tree
*hymenocyphus fraxineus* – ash dieback.
It was all just a joke, a god who didn't exist
upside down in a tree that was dying.
There were creatures beneath it gnawing the roots.

I felt them and heard them but I couldn't see them
though I was witness to the end of the world.
I saw day extinguished. I saw the sun going down
but the lights not come on in your city.
Then the lights in your city came on.

# SOLSTICE FISH

It's night now in blobs and patches
and our houses' eyes are glazed
with peach and nectarine
though the doors are wide awake.

Somehow we are under water
but still breathing in this late
long time of meadowsweet,
rooks in close-cropped fields.

And up where Friday drains away
midsummer fish are cruising
like deep-sea seraphim.

May they save us all before
our heavy metals drown us
or we forget our santería

of wings and scales, of finches
willowherb and meadowsweet.

# INSECTS AND SPIDERS II

*Hatchlings*

They come like bubbles in dough
seething from a folded leaf

dots in thousands that swim out
then evaporate into cracks and holes.

But already by our unswept Septembers
they will be making nets that catch the light.

And if the garden walls and fences fall
or if all the walls are overgrown

a barm of spiderlings will ooze
from splitting stiches all the same

will shelter in cracks or float
downwind downstream from here.

*Wasp mid air*

In the black and yellow plates
of your waisted fuselage,
and your gyroscopic
advance-withdraw-advance,
you are neat as a samurai.

But they do not love how you
hang and zigzag on one tune,
the flamboyance of your antennae
or how your almost prim mandibles,
can make a paper fortress.

My book, admittedly quite old now
even calls you imperfect female
as if your chromosomal balance
had been tilted out of true.

For myself, I salute how you juggle
globes of dew on early mornings
unerringly find sugar anytime.

And this overheated summer I hope
for a fat plummy autumn when you
and your sisters will dance on fruit.

## Bumble-bee in a sunflower

You serve them well, gatherer-valkyrie
voyager-horticulturalist.

You flew light years from the hedge-castle
to weigh your fur down with sweet dust

then find the way on the lines in your mind
across deep space, a row of peas, the road

to feed the queen's children once again
but in a month or so to die in the cold.

So rest here on the surface of this sun.
They won't miss you yet.

*Late sweetness*

At this time of year they go crazed
with sugar-hunger, and the drones
are all most likely dead.

So wasps and bees, inaudible
above city-centre traffic,
latch on to any late sweetness

for instance in the bushes
spilling over these walls along
a former-churchyard path

where at least one man leant
last night on his way through
to piss in the semi-dark.

Today is almost gold
like a two-pound coin found
on a long stretch of paving slabs

and half like summer was, except
only at this time of year
does ivy smell of honey.

*True beetles*

A rosechafer is a box of clockwork
with head and feet the movements of a watch
showing from underneath a lacquered case.
It tick-tocks green-blue as it winds in deep
towards the heart of a rose. It flashes
as it motors through a thistle or air.

No other true beetle purrs through the air
turning up as this does like clockwork
in July, or that you might say flashes.
So if one long evening you stopped to watch
stag beetles flying straight into the deep
they'd be unchanging black in every case.

They are all vanishing in any case.
Our dominion on earth was all hot air.
We went too far, too high, got in too deep.
Why didn't we stop at clockwork?
The tip-tapping in our heads is death watch
chewing through. No wonder we see flashes.

The night sky is stiff with beetles, flashes
and gods who gave up on our hopeless case.
Crabs dogs fish-tailed goats creep and crackle, watch
unconcerned with the burning in our air
the unwinding of our stuff, our clockwork
the sinking of our filth into the deep.

Our leaking ship of fools is out too deep
unships ballast as it smokes and flashes.
Remember how it once ran like clockwork
when museums kept beetles in a case
and shining insects thickened twilight air?
All going down, abandoned on our watch.

Both true and untrue beetles as we watch
are in decline, but still burrow in deep
like doubts. And still puttering through the air
a rosechafer colour-shifts and flashes
settles and then shuts its metallic case
of elytra, shields its wings with clockwork.

We'll watch as the world flickers and flashes
in now too deep perhaps in any case.
A clockwork beetle rumbles through the air.

# THEY WILL

Yes, sycamores will shoot through tarmac
beavers will shift cast-iron drain covers
dam side streets and lanes close to rivers.
Yes, superstores will choke with ivy
herds of cattle will crash through the high street
and shopping malls become impenetrable
with dog roses, blackthorn, and brambles.
You will hide out in roofs and basements
and though fearful of lynxes or bears
will creep out on hot afternoons to the road
to forage for nettles and berries.
Prepare for sidings and industrial units
to go under weed and rising tides,
their gear to seize up and drown in its housing
for pylons and masts to be tangled by creepers
to blacken at evening with roosting starlings.
And will storms come to the bus station
where you've made camp, blow buses over
and clutch the hearts of towns in winter
till there's nothing to see from the suburbs?
Will they shoot you if you get too close
if they've got ammunition to spare? For sure
they will, and nail you to a door as a lesson
of what thieves can expect in that postcode.
And yes, all manner of saviours will come
with a sword or a book and some patter
will promise you a city in the sky
in the west, the east, or an ocean before us
while the cities behind go under
tendrils of growth and clouds of bright insects.
Then skylarks will nest in grass on runways,
and high-rises become black and white cliffs
stiff with guillemots gulls and their guano.

# A SAINT SETS OUT FOR A STAR

When the world is not round
the sky is sea, the sea is sky.

When your habitation is an island
no bigger than a sandal or a hand

it hardly makes a difference
if it's a whale after all.

And when the wind can drown you
water light and air become one tide.

You could still be out there
riding on the pulse and hiss

spinning through the crash and dazzle
in a hide and willow basket.

You'll be needing strong arms though
to reach the evening star.

# TOWARD EARTH-2

As our book will say if we ask
'Though doubt can eat us from inside
certainty is sometimes a sickness too.'

Were the calculations correct?
Is Sun-2 truly red-yellow?
Will our seeds be viable?

Such questions will never leave you.
Your exercises and diet
your meditation and research

will only help you to face them
to accept that you and I
will not touch new ground in this life.

Perhaps your children's children will.
Though they'll be gangling strangers then
no longer trusting our stories

of elephants, seas of wild fish
of food growing green at our feet
periods of time that had names.

And for myself, I spend too long
in the veg-labs, sometimes weeping
when the machines there sound like birds.

Let's sit for a while and listen
to the deep note in the engines
propelling us through this dark heart.

# YOUR SWIMMING TOWEL

It would hardly cover you now
while you dripped in the boys' changing room
among the other half-dressed kids
chattering about how far you'd swum.

5 metres, a smiling blue whale
your first official width
the zig-zag stiches round it
done on your mum's sewing machine.

10 metres, me and another dad
in the echoey splash
watching the lesson. 25 metres
a whole length, a graduation.

400 metres is a whale shark
or something far from the shallow end.
You front-crawled head down then
beyond badges and coloured stars.

This towel was hung on the washing line
still smelling of chlorine, every Saturday.
I'm sorry we haven't been swimming lately
but I'd only be floundering behind you

with the other dads while you swam,
your beard full of fish, like Neptune
out among whales, dolphins
and all the other constellations.

# UNDER ARCTURUS

Day has come inside the walls,
dogs two doors down
are loafing on a savaged lawn.
I came out here to see
higher miles clarify
then monster gates of fire
but find I'm watching
moths and bathroom windows
orbiting a tree.

Now though, Arcturus
is over us. Shaded petals go
ultraviolet, are half ghost
as night-cats step across
ponds of yellow lamplight
to tap our books our brains,
as soundless counterpoint
sends a two-halved moon
arcing through the leaves.

And now in the emptied air
cities are burning out among
unseen towns, depleted stars.
The dogs get whistled in.
An ambulance flies
howling through the sky.
A down-the-middle moon
shivers in its half house
underneath our tree.

# A RAILWAY SPECIAL

Being still stoned from the night before made breakfast
the toughest shift in The Railway kitchen circa 1976.
But if you broke a yolk, there was a bowl of grated Cheddar
next to slices of bread painted with microwaved butter
and stacked on the worktop for lunchtime sandwiches.
So as you cracked another egg into the pan, you'd drop
your misjudgement on a slice, sprinkle cheese, fold and eat it
one-handed. Last night's sex or ceaseless talk and music
would be looping through your brain, the next tide already
rustling the pebble beach behind the houses across the street.

No waves this Saturday rattle the eggs I have gently destroyed
though the pan is hefty and singing in my sleepy grip for you
and dried thyme leaves like grey-green bees spin and fizz
as cheese subsides in squares, undoes itself here in the heat.
In remembrance then of yellow and crispy white emergencies
the fish-slice deals out twin incarnations, which I salt and shut
then cut across with a knife that's quick as a wrasse in a pool.
And though in our road the houses echo no tide behind them
but run downhill alongside their lanes, our table is level,
morning is late today, and 1976 is all over our fingers.

# TRAIN IN YELLOW

You watch cows speeding backwards on long flat miles
underneath stretched out yellow woodlands

watch sheep gliding to a halt when a concrete platform
and a level crossing slide towards you

see them shrinking back to where you started from
along curving land on both sides of the river

and notice how your face is peering in
from coloured hills and pale counties loose above them

how farm machinery and churches turn away behind
the hedges, how sparrows blow about like sparks there.

It's gone, that attenuated countryside, when a bridge
goes over in a moment of forgetfulness

when a tunnel comes upon you like amnesia
and you re-emerge between repeated gardens

in a town on the outskirts of your destination.
The afternoons are getting shorter now. You stop

alongside fenced-off works and numbered sheds
an hour from where you were but not quite at the station.

There is a spattering of yellow leaf among the signs
electrics and redundant track on either side.

# WALKING THROUGH A HALF OPEN BOOK

The playing field was dull green and luminous grey
where I walked across a muddied halfway-line, not stopping
to think I'd never learned the rules. And I became
a ghost to myself as the scripts of trees at the margins blended
into the fog of this January afternoon.

I turned left on a page of tarmac where all the lines
the lights, the paragraphs of dwellings, services and stores
went north to a junction where night had not long arrived.
Was it just last summer, I asked myself, or the one before
that along this way hedges dropped amber dust.

Then I saw it, as clear as the present, a right hand page
where summer rolled slowly downhill and under cars
parked half on pavements littered with privet flowers,
the evening fat as blackbirds, bright as their chimney stacks,
loud as sparrows on walls and kids playing out.

This winter now, as then, I came to the page of our door.
I let myself in to stories I knew and some I didn't,
to opposing seasons in different rooms, our pasts in boxes,
cupboards full of disguises, the kitchen of lists and jars.
And upstairs I found you asleep in a half open book.

Sometime much later I woke beside you,
the hour enormous, every thought branching, no margins,
and out on an unnumbered sheet, no creature no word.

# THIS PAGE HAS BEEN DELIBERATELY LEFT BLANK

In case there should be any confusion
in case you say to yourself
is this some art-work or Zen paradox

this page has been deliberately left blank

So please do not write on it
attempts to do so may result
in marks being deducted, claims rejected
petitions going unanswered

For the avoidance of all doubt
doodling or descent into labyrinths
please leave this page now
Thank you for your co-operation